STANDARD GRADE MODERN STUDIES

Changing Society & Social Issues in the UK

Paul Creaney and Graeme Pont

Editor: Frank Cooney

QUEEN ANNE HIGH SCHOOL
A28

AN HACHETTE UK COMPANY

Acknowedgements

The Publishers would like to thank the following for permission to reproduce copyright material:

Photo credits

Page 1 © Design Pics Inc./Alamy; page 3 © Bernat Armangue/AP/Press Association Images; page 9 © colinspics/Alamy; page 10 © Noam/Fotolia (top), © Photofusion Picture Library/Alamy (bottom); page 11 © Vgstudio/Fotolia (top), © vario images GmbH & Co.KG/Alamy (bottom); page 12 © Alexander Raths/Fotolia.com; page 14 © Jupiter Images/Thinkstock/Alamy; page 15 © Peter Bowater/Alamy; page 16 © Yuri Arcurs/Fotolia (top), © Design Pics Inc./Alamy (bottom); page 17 © Nordicphotos/Alamy; page 19 © Mira/Alamy; page 22 © James Steidl/Fotolia; page 24 © mediacolor's/Alamy (left), © Paul Baldesare/Alamy (right); page 27 © 2006 TopFoto/Matassa; page 30 © www.dundeecity.gov.uk/natentcard (top), © Community Transport Assocation/John MacDonald (bottom); page 33 © Age Concern and Help the Aged in Scotland; page 34 © Moodboard/Fotolia (right), © Tomasz Trojanowski/Fotolia (left); page 36 © Photodisc/Getty Images (top), Brand X Pictures/Photolibrary.com (middle), © Doug Houghton/Alamy (bottom); page 37 © Photofusion Picture Library/Alamy; page 40 © Derek Mitchell/Alamy; page 42 © Comstock Images/Photolibrary Group Ltd (left), © Rob/Fotolia (right); page 43 © moodboard/Corbis (top), © UK Stock Images Ltd/Alamy (left), © Profimedia International s.r.o./Alamy (right); page 48 © JupiterImages/Brand X/Alamy; page 50 © mihaicalin/iStockphoto.com; page 51 © Nicky Saunders; page 61 © Janine Wiedel Photolibrary/Alamy; page 62 © Janine Photolibrary/Alamy; page 67 © imagebroker/Alamy; page 68 © Sumnersgraphicsinc/Fotolia; page 71 © Chuck Eckert/Alamy (top), © Grischa Georgiew/Fotolia (bottom); page 72 © Derek Mitchell/Alamy; page 75 © Paddler/Fotolia; page 76 © John Stillwell/PA Archive/Press Association Images; page 77 © Inclusion and Child Poverty Action Group (top), © www.shelter.org.uk (middle), © www.cpag.org.uk/scotland (bottom); page 78 © imagebroker/Alamy; page 83 © Keith Fergus/ Scottish Viewpoint; page 89 © Hodder Gibson; page 91 © Matthew Fearn/PA Archive/Press Association Images; page 93 © RubberBall/Alamy; page 97 © www.purestockX.com; page 99 © Ace Stock Limited/Alamy; page 100 © Lothian and Borders Police; page 101 © Neighbourhood Watch (top), © Lothian and Borders Police (bottom); page 104 © Stuart Conway/Scottish Viewpoint; page 105 © Andrew Milligan/PA Wire/Press Association Images; page 108 © Dennis Van Tine/ABACA/Press Association Images

Acknowledgements

Every effort has been made to trace all copyright holders, but if any have been inadvertently overlooked the Publishers will be pleased to make the necessary arrangements at the first opportunity.

Although every effort has been made to ensure that website addresses are correct at time of going to press, Hodder Gibson cannot be held responsible for the content of any website mentioned in this book. It is sometimes possible to find a relocated web page by typing in the address of the home page for a website in the URL window of your browser.

Hachette's policy is to use papers that are natural, renewable and recyclable products and made from wood grown in sustainable forests. The logging and manufacturing processes are expected to conform to the environmental regulations of the country of origin.

Orders: please contact Bookpoint Ltd, 130 Milton Park, Abingdon, Oxon OX14 4SB. Telephone: (+44) 01235 827720. Fax: (+44) 01235 400454. Lines are open 9.00–5.00, Monday to Saturday, with a 24-hour message answering service. Visit our website at www.hoddereducation.co.uk. Hodder Gibson can be contacted direct on: Tel: 0141 848 1609; Fax: 0141 889 6315; email: hoddergibson@hodder.co.uk

© Paul Creaney and Graeme Pont 2009
First published in 2009 by
Hodder Gibson, an imprint of Hodder Education,
An Hachette UK Company,
2a Christie Street
Paisley PA1 1NB

Impression number   5 4 3 2 1
Year   2013 2012 2011 2010 2009

All rights reserved. Apart from any use permitted under UK copyright law, no part of this publication may be reproduced or transmitted in any form or by any means, electronic or mechanical, including photocopying and recording, or held within any information storage and retrieval system, without permission in writing from the publisher or under licence from the Copyright Licensing Agency Limited. Further details of such licences (for reprographic reproduction) may be obtained from the Copyright Licensing Agency Limited, Saffron House, 6–10 Kirby Street, London EC1N 8TS.

Cover photo ©Adrian Sherratt/Alamy(left), ©Photofusion Picture Library/Alamy (centre), ©Lihee Avidan/Getty Images (right)
Illustrations by Roger Fereday (cartoons) and Pantek Arts Ltd
Typeset in Stone Serif 11/14pt by Pantek Arts Ltd, Maidstone, Kent
Printed in Italy

A catalogue record for this title is available from the British Library

ISBN-13: 978 0340 987 537

Contents

Chapter 1	Elderly People in the UK	1
Chapter 2	The Needs of Elderly People: Housing and Health	9
Chapter 3	Differences in Wealth, Status and Life Chances	23
Chapter 4	Who Can Help to Meet the Needs of Elderly People?	26
Chapter 5	Unemployment: the Problem and its Causes	34
Chapter 6	Meeting the Needs of Unemployed People	40
Chapter 7	New Technology and Employment	50
Chapter 8	Family Life Today	53
Chapter 9	Making Ends Meet	59
Chapter 10	Poverty: Causes and Consequences	68
Chapter 11	Health and Society	78
Chapter 12	Crime and Law in Society	91

Chapter 1

Elderly people in the UK

What you will learn:

1. The reality of being an elderly person in the UK.
2. The stereotyped images and attitudes people can have of elderly people.
3. The social and economic issues facing many elderly people.

Who are the Elderly?

'Old age' and 'Retirement' are often used interchangeably. These terms do not, however, mean the same thing. In 2009, the retirement age for men was 65 whereas for women it was 60. However, this is going to change from the year 2010 onwards. Throughout this book the term 'elderly people' will refer to those aged 65 or over.

The number of elderly people in society is growing and, increasingly, private companies are showing an interest in catering for the so-called 'grey pound'. Elderly people will, as the years go by, constitute a larger and larger proportion of the population (see Figure 1.1).

What is even more interesting is the fact that within the elderly group, the number of people who are living to an extremely old age, i.e. the age group 75+, is increasing, with numbers set to go up at an even faster rate than at present (see Figure 1.2).

It is clear that in Britain we have an ageing population and that this trend is a growing one. Almost a third of the population will be drawing state retirement pension by the year 2030, with more than one in ten of those being over 75. By 2032, life expectancy is forecast to have risen from the existing 77 years for men to 78 years and for women from 81 years to 83 years. These projected figures indicate that society will need to adapt and change to meet the varied needs of the elderly group.

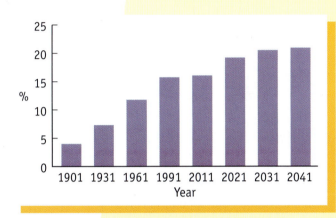

Figure 1.1 Percentage of the population in Great Britain aged 65+, 1901–2041

Chapter 1 — Elderly people in the UK

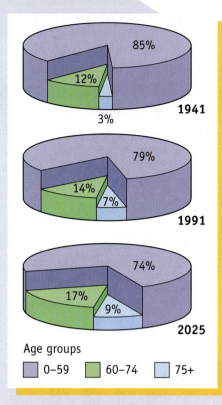

Figure 1.2 The changing composition of the population in Great Britain, 1941–2025

Facts about the Elderly
- There are 11.1 million elderly people in the UK out of a population of 60 million (18.5 per cent). In Scotland there are 958,000 elderly people out of a population of just over 5 million.
- Over 80 per cent of elderly people voted in the 2005 General Election compared with about 45 per cent of those aged 18–24.
- One of the most successful touring rock bands in 2007 was the Rolling Stones. Each band member is aged over 60.
- The richest rock star in the UK is Sir Paul McCartney whose fortune has been estimated after his 2008 divorce at around £600,000,000 He fathered his youngest daughter in his 60s.
- The 2001 census revealed that 8100 people in the UK were aged 100 years or over.
- The proportion of elderly people in the UK is projected to rise to 12.2 million of the population by 2011, then rise to 13.9 million in 2026, reaching 15.2 million in 2031.
- Current average life expectancy at birth is 77 years for men and 81 years for women. Average life expectancy at birth is likely to continue to increase into the foreseeable future, thanks to medical advances.
- When questioned on their lifestyles, 97 per cent of elderly people said they did housework, 69 per cent hobbies and games, 92 per cent reading, 74 per cent travel, 92 per cent watched television and 4 per cent undertook paid work.

FACT FILE

Social Lives of the Elderly

- In the 65–74 age group, 18 per cent of men and 34 per cent of women live alone. At age 75+ the figures are 29 per cent of men and 60 per cent of women.
- In the 75+ age group, 28 per cent of men and 62 per cent of women were widowed.
- 63 per cent of people aged 65–74 and 72 per cent of people aged 75+ have a longstanding illness.
- Elderly people are less likely to have access to a car than the general population and rely more on public transport. Of those aged 65+, 48 per cent do not have access to a car, which compares with only 23 per cent in the 45–64 age group.
- 26 per cent of elderly men and 25 per cent of elderly women smoke. This is a lower percentage than for the general population.
- 250,000 elderly people have no family or friends and 1.29 million feel lonely. 19 per cent of elderly people who live alone will go more than a month without seeing any family member and 9 per cent will go more than 6 months.
- 88 per cent of elderly people living alone have central heating compared with 93 per cent of all households.
- 14 per cent of elderly people have 'mobile' phones compared with 84 per cent of all households.

Elderly people in the UK

Chapter 1

FACT FILE

Economic Lives of the Elderly

- Where the head of a household is elderly, a higher proportion of money, 28 per cent, is spent on housing, fuel and food than for all households at 20 per cent. Elderly people who live alone spend 42 per cent of their income on these items.
- 21 per cent of elderly people in 2006 were defined as living in poverty by the Department of Work and Pensions. This figure remained unchanged from 2005. This means that 2.2 million elderly people were living on 60 per cent or less of the average wage.
- There has been no change in the 11 per cent of elderly people who live in extreme poverty which means living on 50 per cent or less than the average wage.
- Many elderly people experience extreme fuel poverty. 48 per cent of fuel poor households are elderly.
- 35 per cent of houses classified as 'below tolerable standards' are occupied by elderly households.
- 55 per cent of elderly people who own their own homes no longer have a mortgage.
- In the UK, 25 per cent of households in the general population have an income of approximately £600 a week, but amongst elderly households the proportion is four per cent.
- 90 per cent of elderly people need some kind of repair to their homes.
- The wealthiest 20 per cent of UK elderly people have never been so wealthy.

ACTIVITIES

1. Using the Facts about the Elderly information on page 2 describe the advantages and disadvantages of being elderly.
2. Study Figures 1.1 and Figure 1.2.
   Describe the trends shown in the graphs.
3. What explanation can you give to explain the trends shown?
4. Using the information in the Fact Files about the economic and social lives of the elderly, answer the following question:
   - Provide arguments for and against the view that elderly people face a number of social and economic problems. Overall, which view is best supported by the evidence?

What is it Like to be Old?

If someone asked you, 'What is it like to be young?', the answer you gave would probably be quite different from other responses in your class. Why? The reason is obvious – we are all different. The experience of one young person is different from that of another. Similarly, no two elderly people are identical. For every housebound 65 year old there is one who can run a marathon: for every lonely, ill 70 year old, there is one who has a full social calendar. However, as social scientists, we need to look at research, examine trends and probabilities and draw broad conclusions which are true for most elderly people.

Chapter 1 — Elderly people in the UK

Prejudice

Many elderly people face prejudice in all areas of life. As with any prejudice, individuals become unimportant and it is the group to which a person belongs that matters. For example, regardless of how successful, fit, happy and healthy an elderly person is, he or she will encounter severe problems when confronted by a prejudiced person with ageist views. Like a racist who has negative views about all people from particular ethnic backgrounds, an ageist holds negative views about all elderly people.

At a local level, Elderly Forums enable their members to become more aware of their rights and help them to organise themselves in an attempt to get local councils, health authorities and the national government to act.

There is the same variety of personality types amongst elderly people as there is amongst the young. The same is true regarding health, social and economic circumstances.

Elderly people are simply young people who have grown older. Elderly people take into their retirement years the legacy of their lives: their social class; their wealth; their health; their eating and fitness habits; their relationships with friends and family. They also bring a rich experience of life with opinions formed from years of trial and error and having lived through a wide variety of changes.

The Social and Economic Needs and Problems faced by Some Elderly People

Elder Abuse

The pressure group *Action on Elder Abuse* campaigns to help elderly people who are being abused and to highlight an issue which is often ignored. *Action on Elder Abuse* provides leaflets and advice and raises awareness about the abuse of elderly people. It encourages education and research, providing information to a wide range of groups. It also operates 'Elder Abuse Response', which is a confidential telephone helpline. Five main types of abuse have been identified:

- Physical: e.g. hitting, pushing or even deliberately giving the wrong type of medicine.
- Psychological: e.g. shouting, swearing, frightening, ignoring or humiliating a person.
- Financial: e.g. stealing or committing fraud to access a person's money, goods or property.
- Sexual: e.g. a person is forced into a relationship or activities that are not their choice.
- Neglect: e.g. being deprived of adequate food, heat clothing or essential medicines.

The largest group of abused elderly people, 22 per cent, is those between 80 and 84. Over 50 per cent of abuse is carried out on those aged over 70. Identifying abuse can be difficult because the victim often feels embarrassed or even guilty. Often the abuser is a spouse or family member and the victim fears reporting the abuser because of this. Some elderly people do not recognise that what is happening to them is abuse.

Age Concern Scotland estimate that between 50,000 and 90,000 of elderly people living in their own homes in Scotland may suffer at least one type of abuse. They estimate that 40 per cent of elder abuse victims suffer from more than one form of abuse. 75 per cent of reported abuse is against women.

Who Commits Elder Abuse?

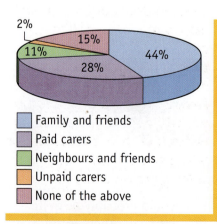

Family and friends 44%
Paid carers 28%
Neighbours and friends 11%
Unpaid carers 2%
None of the above 15%

Source: Action on Elderly Abuse

Elderly people in the UK

Chapter 1

The police will assist any elderly person who reports an allegation of abuse. An organisation called Victim Support should also make contact shortly after the police have been contacted. Victim Support will offer advice, and ensure that the elderly person is being cared for and will provide emotional support, up to, including and after any court case.

Age Discrimination

Laws banning age discrimination in the workplace came into force on 1 October 2006. The government wanted people to have the right to work longer, particularly as we are living longer, healthier lives. But it was worried that the ageist attitudes of some employers were stopping people from doing this.

How the Law Works

It is now unlawful to discriminate against an employee under the age of 65 on the grounds of age. Employers cannot specify that a new recruit should be above or below a particular age. In addition, employers who sack workers or deny them the same training opportunities as their colleagues on age grounds are breaking the law.

The law does not, however, apply to workers over the age of 65. Workers only have the right to request an extension of their working years. If an unemployed person is turned down for an interview because of age, Job Centres will stop advertising the firm's vacancies. The New Deal programme will also be used to help older unemployed people get a job.

ACTIVITIES

1 What problems has Action on Elder Abuse discovered about the ways in which some elderly people are treated?

2 How does Action on Elder Abuse try to help elderly people?

3 What conclusions can be made about:
- elderly people most risk of abuse
- the types of abuse committed
- who is most likely to commit abuse?

Remember: you must state and then justify each conclusion.

4 What are the strengths and weaknesses of the laws banning age discrimination?

Fuel Poverty

Fuel Poverty is a situation where a person does not have enough money to heat their home properly. For many elderly people, low income and poor housing combine to create Fuel Poverty. Where a person is fuel poor they spend more than 10 per cent of their income on fuel bills. Extreme Fuel Poverty is when a person needs to spend more than 30 per cent of their income paying fuel bills.

Living in a low temperature has a direct effect on health. The recommended temperature for a living room is 21°C and 18°C for other rooms. However, a number of recent surveys have shown that many elderly people are living in room temperatures of below 12°C and in extreme cases as low as 6°C.

When exposed to the cold, elderly peoples' body temperature falls greater than in the young, which can lead to hypothermia. This means that the body cools down so much that death can follow if medical treatment is not available. In 2005, 2760 more elderly people died in the winter than during the summer. Influenza contributes to this increase, but so does the effects of fuel poverty.

Chapter 1 Elderly people in the UK

In 2001, the Scottish Government changed the Housing (Scotland) Act to provide central heating for all elderly households which did not have systems installed. Every local council must now have plans in place to tackle fuel poverty. However, in late 2004, 4.5 per cent of elderly households had no central heating.

With the huge rises in oil and gas prices in 2008 and these rises are likely to reappear in the future, fuel poverty is a problem that is unlikely to disappear. In fact it could well get worse.

National Government Winter Fuel Payment

Every household, which includes someone aged 60 or more, gets a Winter Fuel Payment to help towards fuel bills. The payment depends on the age of the people living there. In 2008, for a household with someone over 60 living there, it was £200 plus a one-off additional payment of £50. For those who were 80 or over, the household received £300, plus a one-off additional payment of £100.

The Winter Fuel Payment is designed to encourage elderly people to heat their houses adequately during the coldest months, free from the fear that they will not be able to pay fuel bills.

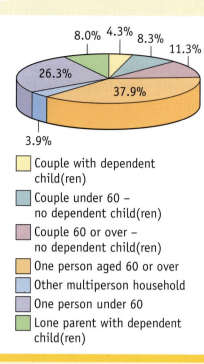

Figure 1.3 Percentages of those living in fuel poverty

FACT FILE

Fuel Poverty

- Elderly people are more likely to be fuel poor than other groups (see Figure 1.3).
- 21 per cent of small elderly households are fuel poor.
- 37 per cent of single pensioner households are fuel poor.
- The very old suffer most from extreme fuel poverty. Only 1 per cent of those aged 25–39 are in this category, but the figure rises to 8 per cent where the head of the household is aged 75+.
- 48 per cent of fuel poor households are in the age group 60+.
- Fuel poverty is more likely in private housing. Elderly people who own their own home or rent privately are twice as likely to be fuel poor than those in rented council housing.

Elderly people in the UK

Chapter 1

Getting Around

Elderly people are much less likely to have access to a car than the general population and they rely heavily on public transport. 48 per cent of elderly people have no access to a car at all. Of those aged 60–69 36 per cent do not have a driving licence. 50 per cent of elderly women have no driving licence.

Elderly people are more likely to use buses than any other group aged over 24, so access to, and the ability to get on buses is important. However, in 2005 only one in four buses and coaches in Scotland had low floors, a powered lift or ramp or any other mechanism to assist frail elderly people or those with mobility problems. Those living in rural or outlying areas can face considerable problems because public transport can be infrequent or bus stops a considerable distance to walk to.

ACTIVITIES

1. (a) What is Fuel Poverty?
   (b) What are the effects of Fuel Poverty on elderly people?
   (c) Using the data in the Fuel Poverty Fact File, state and justify three conclusions.
   (d) Study Figure 1.3 on page 6:
       'People under 60 are more likely to suffer from Fuel Poverty.' (Journalist)
       To what extent can the journalist be accused of being selective in the use of facts?
   (e) What is your view of the National Government Winter Fuel Payment? Give reasons to justify your opinions.
2. In what ways do the transport habits of elderly people differ from the rest of the population?

FACT FILE

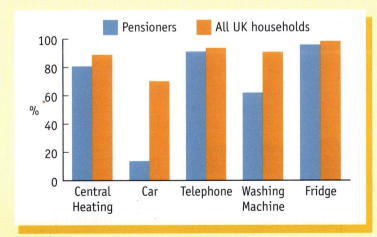

Figure 1.4 The proportion of the population who own basic houshold items (%)

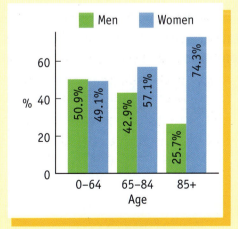

Figure 1.5 UK population by gender

Chapter 1 Elderly people in the UK

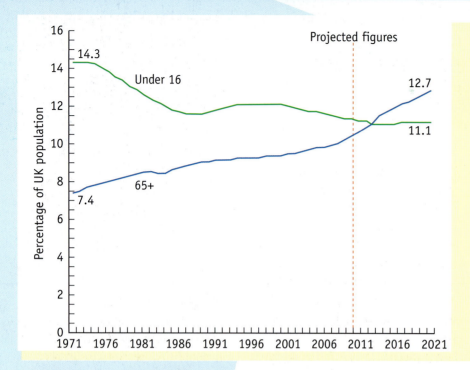

Figure 1.6 Ageing and expanding

UK Population	1961		1981		1991		2001		2021	
	Million	%	Million	%	Million	%	Million	%	Million	%
Total Population	52.8	100.0	56.4	100.0	57.8	100.0	59.7	100.0	62.0	100.0
65–79	5.2	9.9	6.9	12.2	6.9	12.1	6.8	11.4	8.7	14.0
80+	1.0	1.9	1.6	2.8	2.1	3.7	2.5	4.2	3.2	5.2
Total 65+ Population	6.2	11.8	8.5	15.0	9.0	15.8	9.3	15.6	11.9	19.2

Table 1.1 Population projection

ACTIVITIES

Study all the data on pages 7–8.

Write a detailed report in which you include the following:
- patterns of life expectancy and age distribution
- projected rises in the numbers of elderly people
- economic factors relating to the lives of elderly people
- an overall conclusion in which you sum up your main findings and explain the key features you have identified in your research.

Chapter 2

The needs of elderly people: housing and health

> **What you will learn:**
> 1. The housing needs of elderly people.
> 2. The ways in which these housing needs can be met.
> 3. The health needs of elderly people.
> 4. The ways in which these health needs can be met.

Somewhere to Live

The need for housing is one of the basic needs shared by all people. Different types of housing cater for different needs. In addition, the sort of house a person lives in may depend on how wealthy that person is.

The kind of accommodation chosen by people may vary at different times in their lives. For example, early on in life, a couple may find that a flat no longer meets their needs. A larger house with more bedrooms and a garden may be attractive at this stage. Later on, when children have grown up, a large house with its many rooms and high heating costs may not be what is required. On reaching retirement, a number of elderly people review their housing needs.

There are various kinds of accommodation available for elderly people. As a consequence of the rising numbers of elderly people in society, local councils, private companies and voluntary agencies have responded in different ways. Some types of housing are specifically designed or modified to meet the particular needs which some elderly people have.

Surveys have indicated that many elderly people are dissatisfied with their housing, with 25 per cent wishing to move. Many elderly people have homes without an inside toilet or bathroom or even hot water. In general, the housing conditions of elderly people are poorer than those of younger people. One of the main reasons for this is that young people have tended to move into new homes whereas many elderly people have remained in older accommodation with old-fashioned, out-of-date facilities. A worrying relationship is that between poor housing and ill health.

Elderly People and Housing in Scotland

- There are about 660,000 pensioner households.
- About 60 per cent of elderly households own their own homes, 28 per cent rent from councils, 6 per cent from housing associations and 5 per cent from private landlords.
- Approximately 35 per cent of property classified as below the tolerable standard is occupied by pensioner households, and around 20 per cent of such property is occupied by single pensioner households.
- Approximately, 55 per cent of older homeowners have no mortgage.
- Approximately 90 per cent of elderly households require repairs to their properties.
- Very few elderly people live in residential homes or nursing homes.

Chapter 2   The needs of elderly people: housing and health

ACTIVITIES

Using the information about elderly people and housing in Scotland on page 9 answer the following questions:

1. What percentage of elderly people own their own homes?
2. Amongst those who do not own their own homes from whom do most elderly people rent their accommodation?
3. What housing problems do some elderly people face?

The Resident's Story

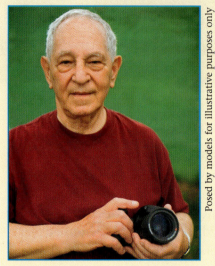

'My name is George Fraser and I was a baker all my life until I retired. I lived with my wife, Mary, in a flat which was part of a tenement block. I really enjoyed living in that flat, but young families moved into the building and the noise became a problem. Also, the flat was poorly insulated and our heating bills were very high. Climbing the stairs was becoming too exhausting and our doctor said that he could help us by recommending to the council that we should be transferred.

To my surprise I got an offer of an apartment in a brand new local authority housing development. I was thrilled! Mary and I have a bedroom, a fitted kitchen, a living room and a bathroom. This accommodation is wonderful and, with many other elderly people in the complex, we soon made a new circle of friends.

I had my doubts about moving out of our old flat with all its memories of the children growing up but with most of our furniture in our new home we feel that little has changed. Sheltered housing is ideal for us.'

Sheltered Housing

Most elderly people are quite capable of looking after themselves and do not require residential care. However, the demands of running a home which has upstairs and downstairs and facilities which have been designed for young or able-bodied people can prove too much for some. One solution to this problem is sheltered housing. These houses are specially designed to meet the needs of elderly people, allowing tenants to live an independent life. There are just below 37,000 sheltered housing places in Scotland provided for rent by councils and housing associations. There are almost 5000 private sheltered housing places.

Chapter 2

The needs of elderly people: housing and health

The Warden's Story

'My name is Ann Banks and I am the warden in the sheltered housing development in which George and Mary Fraser now live. I enjoy working with people so this is a wonderful job for me – even if I can be on call 24 hours a day!

I check on all the residents every morning using my intercom which is connected to each home. I have a chat and ensure that all is well. I have a master key to gain access to individual properties in an emergency, or where a tenant has not responded to his or her daily call.

My job is not to carry out the daily household chores of tenants. If this is required, home helps or family undertake this work.

I know all the tenants well and they feel confident that if they have any problems about their accommodation they can contact me.

Although it is not part of my official job, I get involved in many social events which are held in the games area or in the large social area which is often used for parties or entertainment.'

Posed by models for illustrative purposes only

FACT FILE

Sheltered Housing

What does sheltered housing offer?

Local authorities, voluntary agencies and housing associations are the main providers of sheltered housing. Housing developments can be built as blocks of flats, as houses in terraces or streets or as high-rise blocks. Whatever the style of the development, all are designed with the needs of elderly people in mind. Almost all have the following features:

- They are built on one level so there are no stairs to climb. Where flats or high rise blocks have been built, there are lifts to all floors. Handrails are placed where needed.
- Various communal facilities are available, such as a lounge where tenants can meet and socialise, games rooms, quiet areas and laundry facilities including automatic washing machines and tumble dryers.
- Most developments have a visitors' bedroom so that friends and relatives can stay on visits if they do not live locally or if a resident is ill.
- A TV licence is held by the owners of the developments so no individual licence is payable.
- A 24-hour warden service is there to give help and additional reassurance, fulfilling the role of a 'good neighbour'.

- Heating and power bills are covered by a common charge which includes all costs.
- A two-way intercom links each property with the warden's office, house or administration centre.
- Personal alarms are available to be carried by all residents.
- There are alarms located throughout the property in case of accidents or emergencies and normally the alarms can be operated from floor level.
- Wheelchair access is provided.
- Hand rails are placed in showers and toilets to assist residents, along with bathing aids if needed.

Chapter 2   The needs of elderly people: housing and health

Very Sheltered Housing

In addition to the type of sheltered housing described above, there are a smaller number of complexes called 'very sheltered housing'. These complexes have all the features of the sheltered houses plus a variety of other services which are provided for elderly people who are frail and require further assistance. For example, meals are provided and help can be given with domestic tasks such as general housework. Some care needs are also provided. In 2007, there were 2572 very sheltered dwellings in Scotland.

ACTIVITIES

1. Read the Resident's Story.
   (a) Why did George Fraser wish to move from his tenement flat?
   (b) Give reasons to explain why he and his wife are pleased with their sheltered accommodation.
2. Read the Warden's Story. Describe, in detail, the part played by a warden in a sheltered housing development.
3. Using the Fact File on sheltered housing on page 11, answer the following questions.
   (a) What design features make sheltered housing particularly suitable for elderly people?
   (b) In what ways are the social needs of elderly people met?
   (c) Provide evidence to support the view that 'Sheltered housing provides a safe environment for elderly people'.
4. What is 'very sheltered housing' and how does it differ from normal sheltered housing?

Residential Homes and Nursing Homes

Posed by models for illustrative purposes only

- Getting out to the shops for groceries is too much for me.
- I have no family to help me and I am all alone now.
- Trying to wash my hair or take a bath is very difficult.
- I find it difficult to get in and out of bed myself.
- The house is getting dirty. However will I cope?
- I cannot manage to cook any longer.
- What can I do?

Chapter 2

The needs of elderly people: housing and health

Residential Homes

Some elderly people find that there comes a point in their lives where looking after their own needs is impossible. Normally, the realisation comes over a period of time, rather than suddenly. It is often hard to accept that it is not now possible to do all the housework, shopping, cooking and getting around which you had been able to do until recently. In such circumstances residential care is the most likely option.

Residential Homes are run by local councils, voluntary groups or private companies. They cater for the special needs which some elderly people have.

Normally, a residential home worker is assigned to an individual. This person is called a keyworker. He or she will talk with the elderly person to assess that individual's needs. The keyworker will get to know the likes and dislikes of the person and will find out any problems which may be a cause for concern.

Residential homes will typically offer the following facilities:

- All meals are provided with personal likes and dislikes taken into account.
- Trained Staff are available 24 hours a day with cleaning, laundry and personal help provided.
- The environment is designed to cater for elderly people with strategically placed handrails, lifting equipment in bathrooms, and lounges with specially designed high-backed chairs.
- Lounges where family and friends can socialise with a resident are provided.
- There are visits from hairdressers, the mobile library and health professionals.
- Rooms are for one or two beds and residents can bring some of their own furniture and possessions.
- A variety of social activities are organised.
- Pensions can be collected if required.

In 2007, there were about 32,500 sheltered homes in Scotland owned by Local Councils. In addition, there were 6300 private sheltered homes. Figures for 2005 showed that only 4 per cent of the over 65 age group lived in care homes (residential or nursing homes). There are 1523 registered care homes in Scotland with a capacity to accommodate 38,327 residents. This number has steadily increased over the past 10 years. It is estimated that the demand for places will continue.

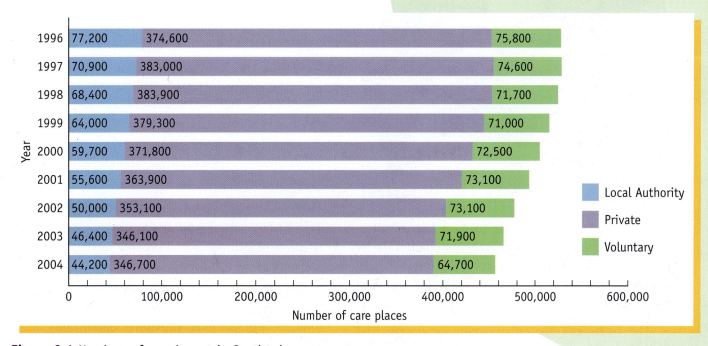

Figure 2.1 Numbers of care homes in Scotland

Chapter 2
The needs of elderly people: housing and health

Nursing Homes

Many nursing homes are run by private organisations. They offer similar facilities to those of residential homes but provide additional support, particularly for those who are suffering from sickness, injury or infirmity. Those in Nursing Homes are usually frail and require constant support.

In addition to the kind of facilities found in residential homes, the following are available:

- Fully qualified nurses on the premises 24 hours a day to attend to residents' needs.
- Specially selected nursing staff who are aware of the needs of elderly people.
- 24-hour 'nurse-call' facilities in each bedroom to ensure prompt attention when needed.
- Assistance with getting around, eating and personal care.
- Assistance with bathing, going to bed etc.
- Specially designed diets to meet any medical requirements which a resident may have.

ACTIVITIES

1. Imagine you are a frail elderly person. Describe in detail the attractions of living in a Residential Home.
2. Read the extract from the leaflet about Residential Homes below. Explain how the social needs of elderly people are met.
3. In what ways do Nursing Homes differ from Residential Homes?
4. Study Figure 2.1. Describe the changes that have taken place between 1994 and 2004.

A NURSING HOME THAT CARES FOR YOU

The nursing home, consisting of three houses set in landscaped grounds, provides accommodation for 64 residents together with day-care facilities for 10 clients. The nursing home will cater for the frail elderly and the elderly with mild mental disability.

- The bedrooms are either single or double and therefore can meet the need for a married couple to share. The single rooms are large in the completely new centre building. A bathroom and toilet are situated between every two bedrooms.
- A nurse call system is installed in every room and registered nurses will be on duty 24 hours a day. Overall supervision will be provided by the fully qualified unit manager and deputy manager/matron.
- Our recreational therapists will provide a range of activities to interest and stimulate the various client groups.
- Regular visits from physiotherapy, dental and ophthalmology practitioners provide a range of supplementary services.
- A hairdressing service will also be available at various times during the week.
- Medical practitioners will provide medical advice and support as required.
- Meals are cooked in our own kitchen by our own very experienced chef. The dining rooms and lounges are spacious, providing opportunity for relaxation after dining.